What others are saying about *The G*

Turning the World Inside-out

In this short but powerful book, Dean Rees-Evans has brought to life the Three Principles as uncovered by Sydney Banks in vivid, real life practicality. His vignettes, involving his loving and wise interactions with young people, on their journey to find there way back to peace, make it clear that the way home is *known*, and only needs to be remembered.

Through Dean's generosity, I am already using the manuscript of this book in my clinical work to facilitate "young people" of all ages, to *remember* and come home to joy, love and understanding.

William F Pettit Jr.
Psychiatrist and since 1983 & Three Principles Student and Sharer

✳   ✳   ✳

Pure Dean, from his own understanding and experience he has written a book of wisdom, love and hope. He lives what he has written. Beautifully said.

Linda Ramus
Vice President of Innate Health Connection, Inc., and long time friend and colleague.

✳   ✳   ✳

If you are a teenager hoping for something more in your life, read this book! It is not that you are missing anything, but maybe very likely you have simply forgotten or never discovered something that is really true about you. Author Dean Rees-Evans is a very unusual and special teacher.

He is one in a million! He can easily teach you to find what you are looking for. Join him in this amazing journey called *"The Great Remembering!"*

Kathy Marshall Emerson
Founding Director, National Resilience Resource Center, USA, and Developing Facilitator of Three Principles Supermind, Educators Living in the Joy of Gratitude webinars.

✻   ✻   ✻

Dean brings the simplicity of happiness to life with his stories of transformation and change. This book demonstrates to teens how simple it can be to awaken to the power they have within themselves to be confident, calm and happy, no matter what!

Christine J. Heath, LMFT, CSAC
Hawaii Counseling and Education Center, Inc.
P.O. Box 795
Pahoa, HI 96778
phone: (612) 702-6539
fax: (877) 831-4232

✻   ✻   ✻

Teens, read this book! Realizing the role thought plays in your life will allow you to uncover the beautiful feelings that lie in your core. As these feelings are released they will guide you through any of the challenges you will face in your life."

Dicken Bettinger
Ed.D., Licensed Psychologist (retired),
Founder of 3 Principles Mentoring

This little book offers a message of uplifting hope, providing a common sense roadmap back home to our natural well-being for youth and others. *The Great Remembering* is a unique way to express what we have forgotten along life's journey, and points us 'home'. The understanding contained in these pages has the power to transform and bring ease back to the life of the reader.

Marika Mayer
Educator and Parent

✳   ✳   ✳

Dean cares and he knows every interaction is important. He shares the Three Principles Understanding with you, so you can find your way. There is comfort in reading about "The Great Remembering." There is inspiration in reading kids say, "don't give up and keep an open heart." Read this book and feel hope. Dean puts you on the path. He will show you the first step—you will always remember.

Christa Campsall
B. Ed., Dipl. Sp. Ed., M. A.
3 Principles Practitioner and author
<u>ed-talks.com</u>
Salt Spring Island, BC, Canada

✳   ✳   ✳

Dean Rees-Evans has a deep and compassionate understanding of the struggles that teenagers face, and he speaks to them in a way they can relate to and appreciate, enabling them to see themselves in a whole new light.

The Great Remembering is a wake-up call for youngsters everywhere to reclaim their creative power and inherent goodness, and to dive into life whole-heartedly, set free from the imaginary prison of their own distorted thoughts about themselves and others.

I recommend this life-affirming book for teens and all those who care about their well-being.

Ian Watson
Founder, The Insight Space
London, UK

The Great Remembering is one of the most calming books I've ever read, and it came to me at the right moment of my life when calm and stillness was what I needed and my heart could hear.

Graham Turner
Graham Turner Coaching
Coaching from the Ground Up

Dean has a nourishing presence about him that leaves its mark on those that come into contact with him. It was with a knowing smile that I read the stories and his simple explanation of the three principles in his first book *The Great Remembering*. The impact that I have felt personally and witnessed professionally from Dean's kind and knowing words has transferred seamlessly to the written form and is sure to leave the same mark on its readers.

Luke Gooding
Team Leader, Family and Community Services, Housing

I am lucky to have Dean as a friend and colleague and am so pleased he has written this beautiful book. He shares and points to some simple and profound truths of how we create our experience moment to moment through our thinking and that we are already whole and perfect in every way. I hope you to take the time to look in the direction that Dean is pointing and see these truths for yourself as true. Dean calls it the *'Great Remembering'* and in knowing and remembering this for yourself, you'll lead a wonderful and fulfilling life and be at your best more often.

James Brett
Founder - Inspire Yourself Now
Sydney, Australia

✷ ✷ ✷

For over three decades, I have witnessed the stories of countless adults who feel imprisoned by low self-esteem, bad luck, and dysfunctional histories. Most of their issues stem from a disconnect with their true power, as they lack an understanding of the intimate connection between their thoughts, feelings and actions. When people reconnect with this power, their lives transform and they wish they had learnt this simple truth when they were younger.

For those who have the good fortune to cross paths with a wise teacher, these simple truths are learned along the way, whilst others struggle, feeling they are fated to be unhappy.

In this fabulous book, *The Great Remembering,* Dean Rees-Evans uncovers these truths for young people in a language that is easy to understand and apply. Within these pages, whatever your age, you will find words from a wise teacher. And you are even luckier if you have stumbled across this book while you have your life before you. I highly recommend this book for all people who are struggling to make sense of a crazy world and feel powerless to do anything about it.

Clare Mann
Psychologist, Communications Trainer and Author of *Myths of Choice: Why People Won't Change and What We Can Do About It.*

The Great Remembering

Turning The World Inside Out

Copyright © 2021 Dean Rees-Evans MSc

All rights reserved

Published by Three Principles Press

All enquiries to: 3PrinciplesPress@gmail.com

Cover and interior design: Carolina Garzón

Editing: Ami Chen Mills-Niam

ISBN: 978-0-9944462-3-7 (paperback)

ISBN: 978-0-9944462-4-4 (e-book)

A catalogue record for this work is available from the National Library of Australia

Dedicated to young people everywhere,

dancing on the light wings of youth.

You are the hope of the world.

For Jess, Donna-Marie, Sammi and Tegan.

Each one a brightly shining star in my heart.

Foreword

The first time I met Dean more than a decade ago, the warmth emanating from his eyes gave me a big clue about the man I would come to know and appreciate.

Dean made an incredible discovery for himself, one that has led him to help young people transform their own lives. Dean awakened to what he calls "The Great Remembering," coming home inside to who we truly are. He "remembered" from that deep and beautiful place within us that we aren't "broken", and nothing inside of us needs fixing. Dean has said it beautifully in this book:

"Inside every human being, including you, there is something so good, and so powerful that nobody can take it away from you. Not by words or by deeds can this thing be damaged; it was there when you were born, and we have it for the whole of our lives, and it is the thing that guides us through life. You could call it wisdom or common-sense, but whatever you call it, it's your birthright."

Dean's experiences with youth span the hemispheres, and the message is identical: human beings have a natural intelligence inside them that lets them know they are truly unbreakable.

This wee book contains much wisdom: the simple and profound truths shared by Dean and the beautiful, transformative stories shared by the young people he has worked with. This book is a treasure to be shared.

Barb Aust BEd, MEd.
Salt Spring Island, Victoria, British Columbia, Canada
January 2021

Introduction

This book is a collection of short stories of extraordinary experiences that I witnessed during my work with teenagers and school students over many years. The book is about offering hope to young people everywhere, where hope may have gone astray. All of my work has been inspired by what I learnt from the lifetime teachings of Sydney Banks, a friend and mentor who uncovered the great gift of the Principles in 1973. He spent the remainder of his life sharing this gift with the world. Sydney Banks had a great love of young people, as do I, and saw them as the hope for the future. He truly believed that it would be the youth of this world that would finally cure the earth of all its ills.

While you read this book, it would not be wise to attempt to gather information that may help you, but instead, simply read it for pleasure. Listening as deeply as you can to the wisdom beyond the words. Enjoy the stories, relax and let your mind open to new possibilities of a better life. As Walter Gropius once said "The mind is like an umbrella – it works best when open." You don't have to read it from cover to cover, you can simply dip in at any page and read a short section and then come back to it again later.

Dean Rees-Evans MSc

Dear Friends,

This is not a self-help book. And by the time you realise what power lies within you, you won't need this book and you will see how you probably don't need help from the outside either, except in certain circumstances, but your own common sense will always guide you. You will know with certainty that you are not broken. In fact, you are unbelievably unbreakable.

The contents of these pages are like a mirror to the wisdom, the natural intelligence in each and every one of us. There is no one person in the world with any more natural intelligence than anyone else. We are everything we have ever looked for in this world. We have all the solutions to any problem that we may face, for our entire life. All this wisdom and common sense is just waiting to rise to the surface of our minds. All we need to do is relax and *let it* happen. We will know when this happens, because we will begin to feel more alive, more ourselves, and more at home as the beautiful human beings that we are.

> *Once while in an exam room I passed a girl who had recently finished her questions. I noticed she was doodling on an extra sheet of paper, on which she had written, "It's just me on my own against the whole world and this is my life." Quietly I asked her in a whisper if she really thought that was true. She nodded. I walked to a nearby piano and wrote a few words on a piece of paper which read:*
>
> "Inside every human being, including you, there is something so good and so powerful that nobody can take it away from us. Not by words or deeds can this thing be damaged. It was there when we were born and we have it for the whole of our lives. It is the thing that guides us through life. You could call it wisdom or common-sense, but whatever you call it, it's your birthright."
>
> *Almost two years later I had the opportunity and good fortune to meet this student again in a classroom. She told me that from the moment she read the words on that note, her thinking shifted away from the thoughts that were creating her darker feelings and lifted her mood. She said that her life changed that day. In her newly uncovered realisation about the role* **thought** *plays in the creation*

> *of all feelings, she felt like she had suddenly awakened from a deep sleep. As her thinking decreased, and her mind was less cluttered with the darker clouds of how she had been viewing her life, she stopped harming herself, both physically and mentally. As her thinking cleared up she began to see the good side of life. She explained how her shift in thinking had helped her family to become closer. This shift in thought also led to deeper feelings of respect for her friends and enabled her to appreciate how her behaviour had been affecting them negatively too. She also explained how she had started going out more with her friends, and having fun, instead of locking herself in her room and dwelling on her depressing thoughts. She realised the huge significance of the simple logical nature of thinking: that whatever "type" of thoughts she may have, they would always lead to that kind of feeling. In other words, darker thoughts lead to darker feelings, and more lighthearted thoughts lead to lighter feelings and a happier and more contented life.*

After we had discussed her shift in thinking, and the changes she had experienced in her life we said our goodbyes, not really knowing if we would meet again. However, she later wrote to me, and shared the following story:

> *"Seeing you again in an English lesson reminded me that I knew you, and that we had met before. I really wanted to tell you that you had changed my life in that exam, when you wrote that note, which gave me new hope for life. After the lesson at the end of school, we had a chat in the English Office, and I explained to you, how one simple thing, like a piece of paper with a few lines on it had changed my life. I know I ended up crying during our chat, because I had never thought of it that way before. I really feel that if that one piece of paper could change my life, then how many other people should read it."*

While working with young people, it is often rare for me to have ongoing communication, beyond the years of school, except in exceptional circumstances. I had the good fortune to meet this former student while on a visit to the British Isles. There was a gap of ten years since we had first met and we planned to meet for about thirty minutes at a coffee shop. Two and half hours later, we were saying goodbye once again.

It was astonishing for me to sit with this now young woman, and witness the light of wisdom that was so obviously shining out of her. She recounted how when she had first started to understand how thought works constantly to create our reality in the moment, that she would sometimes end up losing the nicer feelings and getting lost in darker thoughts again. However, she would always return to that little piece of paper to read, and re-read it in an endeavour to find her way home to nicer feelings again. She said that she had been given a bible and that she kept this note within the pages of the book, and would take it out and read it whenever she was feeling low. She added that she had on many occasions copied it out multiple times in order to try to get to the bottom of how it had helped her so much.

While we sat sipping coffee, this amazing young woman pondered on how her life may have turned out, had we not met that day in the exam when she had been feeling so low in life. We parted company, but before we did she wanted to assure me that she would not be the person she was today if I had not helped her. I reminded her that all I had done was point her in the right direction, back towards the innate health and mental wellbeing that lies within us all: a state of pure consciousness, just below the thin layer of our everyday personal thinking.

The Three Principles

"All three elements – *Mind*, *Consciousness* and *Thought* – are the lifeline to our very existence. It is through these three elements that we have the power to realize the very existence of life." - Sydney Banks from *The Missing Link*

Everything you are about to read can be explained in terms of the "Three Principles" of *Mind*, *Consciousness* and *Thought*.

Firstly, what is a Principle? A principle is a governing law of nature, such as gravity. We do not need to believe in gravity to experience it. Every time we use our balance, such as in dance, or skateboarding, surfing or riding a bike, we experience gravity! If we lean too far, we will fall. We all know that! Likewise *Mind*, *Thought*, and *Consciousness* are *principles* that are always working away in the background of our lives, like an unseen power making life possible. Just as our understanding of gravity has given us the ability to have perfect balance and to fly, equally, learning about the Three Principles sets us free, and raises us up to live a lighter, more loving and happier life.

Put simply, the term Mind is the intelligence behind *all* life. Consciousness is awareness of our existence in the world. Thought is the power that guides us through life.

If any one of these Principles were missing, life would not be possible. Each one weaves its way into who we are, and makes up how we experience our lives, just as they do for all life. Having said this, we don't really need to focus too much on *Mind*, as this is simply the natural intelligence of *all life*, inside of us. And *Consciousness* is simply our awareness of life, because *Consciousness* is what makes our thinking come alive to us, in other words, as we think our thoughts, *Consciousness* makes all them appear real. It is through our *Consciousness* that we experience our thinking. So, in this book we will focus on the role *Thought* plays in our lives.

Are you ready to start looking in a new direction in your life?
Then read on...

The Great Remembering

The Great Remembering is coming home to *who* we really are. This is very simple. We temporarily forget how magnificent we are. When we remember, life becomes simpler. This is not something new. This Great Remembering is a knowing that comes from deep within us, a natural intelligence that we were born with. This is sometimes called common sense or intuition. We all have this wisdom inside and it can never be taken away from us or damaged. Everyone knows in their heart when something is right. It is just that we begin to forget by covering this wisdom up with our thinking about the stuff of life. But just like a precious jewel at the bottom of a deep pool, our understanding is ever present and available to us.

As our jewel-like wisdom comes to the surface of our lives, all sorts of magical things can start to happen. We might find that our relationships with others begin to improve. Our lives become simpler. We see where our feelings are truly coming from, and they lighten up. We start to see that the world is not against us, and that the goodness we feel within us is in everyone around us too. This helps us to feel forgiveness and kindness towards others more of the time.

Even when we are not experiencing a good feeling, and we have become lost in the maze of our minds, the good feeling is always there. It is in the very depths of our being, just below the surface of our thinking. Thankfully, it is only a matter of time before we get back to ourselves again. While things are not feeling so good, we start to intuitively know everything is going to work out just fine in the end. This *Great Remembering* of our own goodness is one of the most beautiful things that can happen to us.

What We Must Know

Yes, that's right. You too! You can begin to live an amazing, beautiful and creative life right now, no matter what you have been through in the past, and how your life has been so far.

What can we know about this Great Remembering? The first thing we must remember is that we are not broken and that there is nothing inside of us that needs fixing. This was the most powerful thing I ever learned in *my* life. Did you know that we were all born with genius, and that we are all as amazing as anyone else we will ever meet or know in this world?

You may never have been told that before, but I am confident that inside you, a certain part of you will know this to be true. Now it is time to come home to who you really are and to live the best life ever.

Living in the *Now*

Whatever we have been through in the past has nothing to do with this moment in time. Every single moment is a new opportunity to see life afresh. Sydney Banks often spoke of living in the present and letting go of the past. Once we do this, our lives change for the better and we find ourselves spending more time being present to the moments of our lives. This present moment in time is the most important thing in life, for as long as we are okay with whatever is happening *now*, our lives will be fine. If we are not okay, wisdom will guide us to something new.

For some children, when they were really young, their thinking was almost completely focused on playing and enjoying life, so they spent their time doing the things they loved doing and very little else. This of course, is not the case for all of us, as we can go through some pretty tough experiences as children. However, whatever we have been through, we can still have a good life now. As we learn to let our wisdom guide us, we can usually stay out of harm's way. But if we need to seek help, then we should.

When we grow older, picking up habits from the adults around us, we start to think and worry about things, about life and circumstances. We may start to experience anxiety about what others think of us. If we do worry about other people's thoughts, there are two things to keep in mind about this. Firstly, we cannot really know what others are thinking about us, and secondly, there is nothing we can do about what they think anyway, because they are their thoughts, so the worry is pointless. Wisdom of course, may lead us to simply act with more kindness towards others whom we think are seeing us negatively. More importantly, it is always *our* thinking in the moment that makes us feel as we do, not other people or their thinking.

Sometimes we might worry about the past, especially the parts we didn't like. And we might start to worry about the future, out of fear of what may come. It is possible for us to create all sorts of scenarios of mishaps and unhappy endings with the thinking of our vivid imagination. The novelist Mark Twain once wrote: "I have had a lot of worries in my life, most of which never happened." Painting the clear picture that we can all worry about a multitude of things during our life, most of which are really not worth the effort, and they are all being created from the power of *Thought*. When our thinking returns to the present moment, it is almost impossible to be bogged down in low feelings of the past or anxiety about an unknown future.

I once met a girl who had been suffering for many years. When she was young, she had been very troubled and her parents, being worried about her, had sent her to see a psychologist, to see if therapy could help. It didn't help, and she continued to struggle with how she felt in life about events from her past. Her ups and downs were just too uncomfortable to bear. I met her when she came to a talk with her mother that I was delivering in Melbourne, Australia.

When she heard about how thoughts create reality, and that "what" she was feeling about her past came from her thinking, and not from the events themselves, she suddenly started to feel better in the moment, as if she had just woken up from a bad dream. When we spoke afterwards, she had a question, "What do I do when the bad stuff comes back?" I laughed and said there really was nothing she needed to do with the 'bad stuff', because it was just coming from thought, and that thought alone could do us no harm. There was much laughter and tears.

Her mother seemed relieved to see her daughter in joy. When things had calmed down, the girl looked at me and said, "But Dean you are so amazing." I laughed again, and asked her what she thought she was looking at? She wasn't sure. I told her that she was looking into a mirror, and all that she thought was so amazing was simply a reflection of herself in the living moment. I told her that when we are present to life, and living in the moment, we are much less likely to be affected by thoughts from the past. After more tears and laughter, the girl returned to a state of calm and peace, as she began to see more clearly where her state of mind had come from. From within, from thinking in the present moment, as it does for everyone. This is not to say that her life became perfect after that, she still had the usual ups and downs of life. She just found that it was easier navigating the downs with some understanding of the role of Thought in her life.

Common Sense

We all have common sense, wisdom and good feelings inside of us that have been there since the day we were born. These forms of thought that arise from wisdom, guide us through life, and nothing can take them away from us. If we can get quiet, even for a moment, and listen to the still quiet voice inside of us, we will remember the magic and wisdom of ourselves.

How will we know if it's our wisdom we are hearing?

That's easy, because wisdom always comes with a good feeling, and feels *right* inside, feels certain. Also, wisdom is free from feelings of confusion, tension, anger and fear. When we listen to this natural intelligence inside of us, we just know that it is right! Everyone does, it is just that sometimes we forget.

> *One day I entered a science lesson, which had only four boys in it and a learning support assistant. During this lesson I met a boy, who I later discovered had a reputation of being unruly at school and that it was very rare for him to stay in a classroom for an entire lesson. This, I was informed, had been his pattern for the whole of high school. This information about the boy was fascinating to me, because when I started speaking about how our thoughts create our life, he became deeply interested, and focused, to the apparent disappointment of his three other class buddies who seemed determined to be disruptive. It appeared that his wisdom woke up in a flash and he remained engaged throughout the entire lesson. I spoke of the simple logic of how our thinking in the moment creates the feelings we have inside us and that the unique circumstances of our lives do not necessarily determine how our life will turn out. I explained that it was common sense that guided us through life, and that in the moments that we could see this clearest; it would become much easier to navigate through tough times in life.*
>
> *When the lesson ended, this young man was still there. The bell rang for break. He thanked me enthusiastically, shook my hand vigorously, and said that I had helped him solve all the problems he had had in his entire life! I later learnt that he left school that day with a deep feeling of enthusiasm for life, and whenever I saw him later during the school year, he seemed to have maintained a good sense of his part in the moment-to-moment creation of his reality. In other words he was accessing common sense or wisdom more of the time. When common sense wakes up, we have an experience of the Great Remembering.*

Coming Home

We all enjoy times when we feel cheerful and carefree for no reason. When we feel at peace in ourselves and relaxed, time seems to pass without us noticing. It feels like we don't have a worry or care in the whole world. At these times, we have fallen back, naturally, into a better feeling state, and our thinking has slowed down. This feeling is like a coming home and a remembering, which always feels gentle, comforting and natural.

This relaxed state is how we were born, and who we really are inside, underneath the sometimes negative thinking we might do about ourselves. This way of being requires no effort or work on our part. This is because feeling calm, relaxed and at home in ourselves, is where our mind wants to be. It is not so much about doing something in order to feel better, but simply being the individual we are, naturally, underneath the layers of our daily thinking.

This feeling is discovering that we are generally okay and fine with the world, most of the time. Because when we are feeling bright on the inside, the world outside generally seems that way too. Even if things in the world do seem difficult and harsh, we begin to understand that our worrying won't help us uncover the solution. Yet, if we are feeling relaxed and at home inside, the answers to our problems will more likely come to us easily. Similarly, whether we feel good or bad, we begin to realise: whatever we feel inside, it is always coming from our *thinking*.

There are also times when we have low feelings, as we go through life's ups and downs. We can end up feeling down and we don't know where the feelings have come from. This happens to everyone, and is what might be called unrecognized or subconscious thinking. A simple way to look at this is to make a comparison with the hardest thing we ever had to learn, which is to walk. Some negative experiences we go through in life can end up becoming buried so deep in our mind that we don't even know we are thinking about that stuff anymore. So, just like we don't need to think about putting one foot in front of the other as we walk, some negative thinking simply becomes invisible to us. The good news is, it won't last. All thoughts we have come and go, and just as you will have noticed, these unrecognized thoughts go too.

One day, I was called to an English lesson where there had been an fight between two boys. One had punched the other. I needed to find out what happened and clear things up. When I spoke to the boy that had done the hitting, he told me how he was always being teased about his size, and had learnt to ignore those comments, but it had gone too far when the other boy had insulted his mother.

We talked about the possibility of not simply ignoring another person's insults, but recognising that the possible reason someone would do such a thing was because they were suffering themselves. He understood clearly that he got himself in trouble through his reaction to the comments of the other boy, but didn't know how to get past the feelings of insult. As we spoke, he was feeling calmer, and seemed certain that he wanted to be stronger in these difficult situations, he just didn't know how. We explored the idea that when insults come, they are not really about our family or us. In other words they are not personal. We spoke about the simple notion that when insults come from others, they are a strong indication of that person's state of mind in the moment. We also spoke of the fact that if people were feeling okay in themselves, they probably wouldn't want to say mean things anyway. The boy seemed to understand. When we are in a good mood, we don't go round being rude or insulting other people, so why would anyone else do that too? The penny dropped, and he said that felt a lot calmer, and understood what he needed to do in order to avoid further confrontations. In other words, he saw the deep significance of the role thought plays in creating his reactions in these potentially conflict-filled situations.

I saw the same boy a few weeks later and checked in with him to see how things were going. I was amazed to find him in very good spirits and feeling self-confident. He looked very much at home and relaxed in himself. In fact, he seemed to have almost completely forgotten the incident and how difficult life used to be for him at school. He had realised how his thinking was creating his feelings, and how these feelings led to his reactions to insults from others. Feeling more at home and laid back in himself, and no longer allowing his 'thought' buttons to be pushed, this young man was in a much more resilient and hardy place to deal with the ups and downs of life at high school. On asking him about the teasing, he simply said, "Oh no. No one bothers me now."

This doesn't mean to say that this boy would never have troubles again. What his response points to is his uncovering of the simple logic that when we see the role thought plays in our and others' emotional responses to the world, we tend to feel more confident and become less reactive; we are more at home in ourselves. This is because it is much harder to see the difficulties of life in the same way when we know the part we play.

Be Gentle

For all our friends and family that have not yet remembered how life works, we must be gentle with them. We cannot force anyone to see what we have seen so far. Just like us, they need to wake up from the dream of this world. The only way we can help them do this is by being as uniquely and genuinely *us* as we can be.

When we are in that space of remembering and understanding, our thinking slows down and this can really help others feel safe and see their wisdom too. We become like a mirror to them and shine back the good feelings and common sense that lie within them. If we can just remain patient with others and stay in our own good feeling as much of the time as possible, we will help them. It is the best gift we can give to those we love, and the greatest gift we can give back to the world.

Many different situations will arise in which we can become the bedrock of hope for our family and friends. A story I was told recently is a great example:

> *It was in the middle of bush fire season in Australia. A family had just heard on the radio that a fire was raging nearby. The blaze was covering some five hundred hectares of land, with the potential of hitting their area and house. As they rushed from one task to the next, preparing the house for the worst, they began to realise just how unprepared they were. They worked busily, and then the eldest daughter decided that she was too hungry to keep going and decided that she needed to sit down and have a meal. Her mother and sister went crazy at her, thinking she was not taking responsibility, or did not care about the coming fire.*
>
> *She told them that, although it was important to be ready, they also needed to look after themselves and eat, adding that it was also important to stay as calm as possible, so that if the emergency reached them, they could make clear decisions about what to do. The girl added that, at the time, although she could see that her mother and sister were distressed, she felt a deep calm inside herself, feeling certain that they would all be okay, which they were. This certainty she felt is what we mean by wisdom, common sense, intuition, a deep, deep knowing or Great Remembering.*

The Happiness That Comes From Remembering

The good feelings we start to experience as a result of remembering who we really are on the inside have their own way of spreading to others around us. This is like throwing a pebble in a pond and watching the ripples spread out gently across the still surface of the water. Our good feelings and a quiet mind become contagious. Our happiness and contentment spreads to others. Just like hearing funny laughter in someone, we cannot help but laugh too.

It was exam time at high school and the students had a double-session art class, despite the fact that they had previously finished their art exam. As the students entered the room, I overheard comments like, "This is going to be so boring!" and "This lesson is really going to drag", and "What are we going to do for TWO WHOLE HOURS?" As the last students filtered in, I suggested we could have some fun exploring certain mindsets that might help them get through the rest of their exams and beyond into their everyday school life. A few kids got really curious, and the feeling in the room shifted from one of low hopes to a sense of excitement and interest. We explored the idea that while exams certainly looked serious and stressful from the outside, due to the expectations of parents and teachers, there may be an undiscovered element yet to see. We looked into the simple fact that it was our thinking and expectations of exams, which created the feelings we experienced, not doing the exam or even being in the exam environment.

I asked the students to consider the possibility of seeing exams as the perfect conditions for the task at hand. In other words, the room would be silent; no one would distract us, or speak to us, and nothing would get flicked at the back of our head. Additionally, while in the exam, we usually have all the gear we need, and if something in our equipment should fail, we only need to raise our hand and we will be provided with a replacement. Also, the simple fact that in order to complete the exam successfully, we are only required to answer questions about what we have studied during the previous term. Or we may be asked to read and interpret a new text, and in the case of art, complete a piece of work in the set time.

The students concluded that if they were able to stay in a calm space within themselves; and, if they could let go of their previous stressful and anxious thinking about exams, they would more likely be able to apply themselves more fully to the exam, and do their best work. This development in the students thinking seemed to create a genuine sense of enthusiasm in the room and an awareness of new hope for tackling exams and schoolwork. These freshly uncovered feelings of happiness and eagerness associated with tasks that had previously been thought of as daunting and stressful was an eye-opener to the students.

I saw a few of these same students some days later in an English lesson. This time they entered the class with a lot more willingness and there seemed to be a real buzz around them. The students were keen to have more discussions around the role of **thought** *and wanted the kids who had not been present to hear it too. They felt that all students could benefit from this understanding of the role that thought plays in the creation of our feelings.*

One young man wanted to share his experience. He explained how he had previously been a very anxious person, and a constant worrier. However, investigating the belief of how our preconceived ideas about many things may simply be 'habits of thought', shifted something deep within him. He said that his thinking had become lighter and more easeful. He found himself feeling less anxious and mostly calm since the art class. What he found fascinating about this shift was that other people around him seemed to be picking up on his newfound relaxed state. He said that friends and classmates wanted to be around him more of the time, like bees around a honey pot, and he was very happy to share whatever he could about what he had understood. The boy's buddies seemed to want to 'get' some of what he seemed to have. This, he said, had rarely been the case before, but he was not complaining.

Like What You Do

When you start to remember how life works, it is not uncommon to start doing the things you love to do more of the time. When you do the things you love spending time doing, you return to a more natural way of being, and usually have less on your mind. It is like resuming a state of playfulness you forgot you used to experience, not unlike a small child happy to play for hours with only sticks, leaves and mud. You simply start to experience more *joy* in your life, naturally.

Conversely, what also happens is that you start to see that the chores of life, like cleaning your room, or washing the dishes after a meal, that you used to find dull and boring, or just didn't want to do, become more neutral to you. They are no longer a task or an unwanted duty; they are simply something that you need to get done. You begin to see that the *thinking* you have been doing about these tasks is what made you feel dissatisfaction with them, not the doing of them.

This shift in thinking can really help you let go of the feelings that are often associated with the undertaking of mundane tasks. This allows you to carry them out with more ease, because when you start to *see* these duties more neutrally, the mind eases up. In other words these responsibilities stop bothering you because your *thinking changes* around them. This frees up a lot of energy for the things you love to do. You could think of it like this: if your mind were like the screen of a radar, many of these tasks or duties would simply stop showing up on the screen of your thinking. You would simply get on with them without concern or hesitation.

Two Types of People

There are only two types of people in this world. There are those, like us, who have started to remember how life works, and are living in nicer feelings more of the time. And there are also those that are *going* to remember, who will also begin to live with restored feelings of hope, love and understanding. When we all remember who we really are, the world will change for the better in an instant. That will certainly be a big day to celebrate!

One of the differences between people that have remembered, and those that have not yet remembered is this: when we remember, we start to see that the bad feelings we are having are simply coming from *our* thinking. It becomes clearer that when those thoughts pass, the uncomfortable feelings will go too. Those who have not yet remembered will still be thinking and believing that these feelings are caused *by* the world. They innocently imagine that their feelings are coming from the 'outside'. They think feelings come from other people, or the circumstances and situations of their lives. We often hear: "He made me mad" or "She got me so upset." Such feelings may look like as if they are coming from the outside, but we begin to see that they are really coming from the *thoughts*, which we have about situations and other people.

This is not to say that sometimes we go through tough situations that we need to get ourselves out of. Life does not become perfect simply because we have seen where our feelings are coming from. However, our wisdom and common sense can really help us to steer our way out of trouble. We can forgive people for being mean, but being kind does not involve being a doormat that people can walk all over. Our true strength lies in knowing when to walk away from others when things are looking like they might get dangerous for us.

On my very first day at a new school, where my duties were pupil behaviour management, I was directed to a classroom to deal with a girl causing problems with the teacher. When I arrived, not even knowing the girl, I received a lot of abuse and swearing from her. The situation was resolved, but due to the nature of the verbal abuse, the girl's mother was called into school. This was an attempt to get to the bottom of her ongoing disruptive conduct and the problems she was causing to a lot of staff and other pupils.

Over a period of a few months, we spent time working together, and it was obvious that she struggled in the school system. She had not been doing well educationally, mainly due to the volatile reactions she had to the pressure she felt she was under. She came from a large family, with many siblings, and seemed to have a difficult and stressful home life. When we spent time together in the classroom, I made sure it was always lighthearted and fun. We focused on her strengths, which helped her see something of her unlimited potential. Some months later, the school and the mother were baffled by her complete turnaround. The school reported that she had been doing well in class, was getting on with her teachers, and applying herself to her studies in a new and agreeable way. This was a real turnaround in her conduct both at school and at home. The staff added that she was a real pleasure to be around, and the girl's mother believed that her daughter had changed so much for the better, that she hardly recognized her.

> *The solution to this mystery of the girl's changes is simple. She started to recognise that her old negative habits of thought about herself were not helping. She had previously believed that she got angry with people and situations because they made her mad. As she started to see the role* **thought** *played in her reactions, she found she had a much greater capacity for her work at school than she had previously believed possible. The girl also found that she could communicate with family, friends and teachers with a lot more ease when her thinking was lighter. She seemed to be seeing life with new eyes, and had lightened up and was enjoying life more. As she did this, every area of her life was affected. When she lived in better feelings more of the time, the old habits of behaviour dropped away as if they had never existed in the first place.*

This is not to say that this girl would never experience difficulties and suffering again. Life for all of us constantly presents challenges. When our thinking slips back into old habits of thought, without us even noticing, we can start to spiral downwards. This can make life feel pretty uncomfortable again. Thankfully, this doesn't last, as we start remembering how *Thought* creates our feelings through the workings of *Consciousness*, and we return to nicer feelings in our day.

Helping Others with Feelings of Hopelessness

Those people who have not yet remembered who they are, or what an amazing capacity for goodness they possess, can create feelings of hopelessness. These same people may begin to feel that there is no obvious solution to the difficulties of life. However, when we remember, we begin to see the world anew, and we reclaim nicer feelings and hope about life again. When we live with a quieter mind, and nicer feelings, it helps us in difficult situations with others, because we can start to get a sense of how the other person is thinking and feeling at that time. We understand that it is *not about us*. In other words it is not *personal*, but their upset informs us that the other person is suffering in some way. This can really help us live in kindness more of the time and more deeply understand others, as we understand how we sometimes get lost in our thinking. This doesn't mean we let people take advantage of us. It just means that we more clearly see where another person's suffering is coming from. It is coming from within;

from the way they are making sense of the world with their thinking, just as we all do.

If we are in this neutral space of remembering, which is a calm and beautiful feeling, we are more likely to be able to help gently resolve the situation for the other person. Or have the calmness of mind to wait until the other person can hear us again, when their thinking has slowed down a little. We may decide that this is not the right time to try and help them. They may not be ready or be able to see that it is only their thinking in the heated moment that is creating uncomfortable feelings. And so, we may need to be patient with them until they are in a more receptive state of mind, where a suggestion from us might become the small spark that wakes them up to living a better life. We all know how difficult life can feel when we lose our bearings and are feeling upset or angry, and so it is always a comfort to us to have friends that have time for us and will listen.

How Do We End Up Forgetting?

There will be days when we forget again, and we can become temporarily lost in the maze of our mind, searching everywhere for answers. The illusion of sadness is so convincing that we feel we need to fix something inside of ourselves in order to feel better. Ironically, we often end up looking for answers on the outside to fix the feelings we don't like on the inside. When in reality there is nothing broken that needs fixing at all. It is just our thinking again. How great is that to know? That thought can be a cage in which we trap ourselves. And because that cage is only made up of our thinking, we can walk right back out again whenever we remember this.

The Great News is Nothing Lasts

When we remember that the way we feel is created via our thinking, we may not always feel better at that exact moment, but we start to understand that these feelings probably won't last. In fact, they can only last as long as we have those thoughts. This is similar to a basic mathematical equation, like two plus two equals four. In other words *Thought*, plus *Consciousness*, equals feelings. However, if we briefly forget that our feelings come from our thinking, we can get caught up in muddled thinking, trying to work out what it is outside of us in the world that makes us feel so bad, and how to fix it! But our feelings don't need 'fixing', because they will change the moment our thinking shifts in a new direction.

Thinking is like a roller coaster ride, it is in constant motion and goes up and down, but eventually we get off the ride, and on to the solid ground of our 'knowing' that our thoughts are what create all our feelings. There are times in life when things happen, like losing a pet or a friendship ends, or someone in the family dies, where we feel naturally sad. These feelings are also coming from thought, but it is completely natural to experience sad thinking around these events. How long these feelings last in us will be different from person to person. This is because we have our own unique way of seeing the events of our lives. However, an understanding of thought seems to help these feelings pass more quickly. But however long they do last, eventually we let go of the sadness and return to nicer feelings, because nothing can last forever. And we end up focusing on all of the good and beautiful memories we have of the person rather than feeling sad.

I once met a boy who attended a research project I was conducting in a high school in Britain. The main purpose of the project was to help raise feelings of wellbeing and happiness with both students and staff volunteers that attended. When I met this young man, he seemed very shy, spoke little and made no eye contact. If he did look up, you could only see one of his eyes as his long black hair hung down over one side of his face, and even this eye contact would be fleeting. His posture often seemed awkward and uncomfortable, and he remained quiet throughout the training and asked few, if any, questions. I have noticed over the years that even when a person is quiet during sessions, or seemingly resistant to what they are hearing, it still seems to helps them begin to understand the workings of the mind, and the huge part thought plays in how we experience our lives.

Later that same year, after the summer holidays, I saw this young man, and at first I hardly recognized him due to his upright posture and confident presence. He seemed like a different person altogether. He stopped me in the walkway, pushed his hair back from his eyes, looked at me directly and put out his hand to shake mine. He wanted to thank me for the training, and make sure he conveyed his gratitude for the changes he had experienced in his life. It had gradually dawned on him that it was his thinking that had been creating his low feelings, not the circumstances of his life. The more he remembered this, the less time he spent in lower moods. After a time, other people around him started to notice his lighter attitude to life. What followed as he began to change and became more relaxed in life was that his relationships with family and friends began to improve.

Life at home hadn't always been easy, but now he could see the part his moods had been playing to the mixed feelings of life with his family. He started to notice how his family members would go into a low mood about something, but that they weren't seeing their feelings as coming from thought. This helped him to become more patient with them and added that things were much calmer at home now.

He admitted that although he was feeling more buoyant in himself, he struggled to say how, or to find the right words to explain it to others. He described how he had found that when he was hanging out with friends and they would talk about the things that were bothering them about life; he would do his best to explain the role of thought and its power to create our feelings. When he spoke to them, despite the fact that he didn't feel he had the language to explain it well; it still seemed to help them too. It was obvious that this young man was feeling deeply grateful for what he had uncovered in himself, and the effect this was having with those around him. His confidence shone out of him like a bright light in the world. It was a magical moment to see him again that day.

The Mystery of Time

Once a moment is lived, it is gone forever. We cannot get these moments of our lives back again and this is what makes life so precious. Therefore, 'the past' is simply a memory, the result of thinking about what has been before. If it is a good memory, we will experience joy in the remembering, like a funny story that seems so much funnier the second time around and we end up belly laughing about it. Or a beautiful memory from a holiday, and spending time with those we love. However, if it is an uncomfortable or sad memory, we may suffer painful feelings while we bring this memory back to life via our thinking. But we can only have these feelings as long as we have those thoughts! Once the thought is gone, just like the moments of our lives, so is the feeling.

Thought has this amazing capacity to carry us out of the present moment of our lives and into the 'memory' of the past. It's a bit like time travel, only the time machine is our own 'mind'. It is interesting to consider that if we had an actual time machine, I don't think we would decide to go back to the bad and upsetting times of our lives, I think we would head straight for the joy and fun times. But sometimes we just don't see these sad or uncomfortable memories as thought, because they are hidden from us, and the past looks *real*, as if it is happening all over again.

Because we are thinking beings, and we think for the whole of our lives, we cannot help *what* thoughts enter our mind, but we do have choice over which ones we give energy and focus to. What is fascinating about the *mind* is that it naturally filters most of what we think throughout the day. This is because a lot of our thinking is not so important to us, so the *mind* simply casts it aside. If the mind didn't work like this, we might go crazy with all that thinking! But as we begin the see the power that lies within us all, to create our experience of life, we are brought back to living more in the *now*.

Ghosts of the Past

When we think of the *past*, we temporarily bring the past back to life again with our memories, which are all just thoughts. The simple fact is that the past doesn't actually exist anywhere except in our minds.

Unhappy memories can begin to haunt us like ghosts. The effects of this kind of thinking are sometimes called 'depression', 'sadness' or 'low moods'. Whatever we call them, they all come from recurring thoughts that have become invisible to us. In other words, we are no longer aware that these painful feelings are created *from* thought. We assume the low feelings are coming from the events of the past themselves, rather than *our thinking* about the past. When we see that these low moods are solely created *from* thought we start to experience the past in a very different way. We take it less seriously, less personally, we lighten up about these memories. Because we see memories for what they really are: just thought, and completely harmless. The past doesn't change, that is impossible, but the way we think about the past shifts, and new light shines on what previously looked like very dark corners of our mind.

When we accept that our bleaker thoughts cannot harm us if we don't focus on them, we also realise that they can't harm anyone else either, if we don't act on them. This is because thoughts simply fade when we are no longer interested in thinking them. Like the ghosts of our past, fading into the bright sunlight of our mind, we begin to experience the joy of living our lives more in the *now*. When we start to live more in the now, we begin to set ourselves free from the uncomfortable or even distressing memories of long-ago. In this newfound freedom from uncomfortable memories, the natural state of joy arises from having less thinking and a calmer mind. Which in turn, leads to us having more energy for all the things we love to do.

Fears for the Future

We all live with our hopes and dreams for the future, this is naturally part of being human. These thoughts can lay the strong foundations for the living of a good, healthy and happy life. Yet, we can also use our creative capacity for thought to fill our minds with fears. Such as, "What if things don't go the way I want them to?" or "What if things go wrong or someone I love dies?" This innocent misuse of our amazing capacity to 'think' literally anything can create incredibly uncomfortable feelings in our lives. However, when we realise that being anxious or worried about the future is no different than having unhappy memories from the past, we can let go of these thoughts too. As we begin to uncover the simple secret of how our *mind* works, this helps us to remember who we really are. We understand that *all* feelings come from our own personal thinking.

When we think about the 'future' this is like a dream, basically made-up from the thoughts we have about the things we would like to do. I used to ask my students a simple question to illustrate this point. I would ask the teens: "If we come back to the same lesson in a week's time when will that be?" The answer would often be: "The future!" then another student would say: "No! next week's lesson, will still be the *now!*" The simple logic of time is, that as each moment is lived and felt by us, and we can never get that moment back again. So we are constantly moving forward into the next moment of our lives and thus, 'the future' never arrives, because it doesn't really exist. We live out our lives in the ever present *now*, moment-to-moment. Knowing this can really help us to stop worrying so much about what might happen.

The present moment of our lives is where the real magic begins, and living in the present allows us to deal with whatever is going on *now*. Understanding this simple truth is one of the greatest secrets in the world. Knowing this sets us free from suffering in the moment. We can get upset or feel down about something in life, yet these feelings will only last for as long as we think them into existence. This is exciting news for all of us!

Keep in mind that when those around us seem moody, they have become lost in their thinking. So, if we just give them space and plenty of love, they will come back to a better feeling again, too.

Slowing Down

When we see how life is created from the inside out, our thinking slows down. When our thinking slows down, we feel better. We return to our natural and familiar good and warm feelings again, as if they never left us.

The best way to think about this is to remember that *we are not just our memories* or *our thoughts of the future*. Hardly! In fact, we continually create our experience anew with every thought we have. This is freeing for us to remember. We are turning the world inside out when we understand that our thinking comes from within us, that thought is what creates our feelings. We start to become less upset when things are not going the way we would like them to. We intuitively know that things always change. We begin to understand that all experiences come to an end, but our innate wisdom and well-being is infinite and this gives us great hope for life!

The following is an extract from a girl mentioned earlier in the book. This section is in her own words:

> *... Ever since that talk, I've never been able to think the same. Suddenly, I was so aware of my thoughts! I began to see things differently. I no longer felt so much resentment and anger for people who, I had once looked down upon. I instead realised they were just acting in the best way they could in that time in their lives with the knowledge they had. I read* The Enlightened Gardener, *by Sydney*

Banks and The Spark Inside, *by Ami Chen Mills-Naim. I can only describe the feeling I experienced like being a jumbled puzzle, transforming into a complete whole with all the puzzle pieces falling back into the right places.*

Then another major turning point happened. I was in my bedroom, when I came across some old books that I had once filled with writing about my bad experiences. I had been told that writing about your issues would help, but really it only made me dwell in them all the more. As I skimmed through the pages, I saw all the same things being written, all the same negative thoughts. I realized how much I had let my thoughts have control over my life, and that it wasn't the events themselves that were burdening me, but the bad thoughts I was having about them! Suddenly, I just wanted to be rid of my past once and for all, and not hold onto it anymore. I had a whole life ahead of me!

The next fire we made at the farm we lived on, I took my collection of papers and burned them. I wondered why I had not let go of them sooner, but I realised this was just all part of my journey and I hadn't been ready until now. As those papers turned to ash, I felt an emptying as I let go. I knew that it didn't mean that these thoughts would never return, but I had let go of my past experiences and when these thoughts did come back, I would be able to be 'the master of my thoughts' and simply let them go.

Today, I feel much more ready to take on the world. This is the stuff they should be teaching in schools! I also know that I still have a lot to learn, but I have confidence in myself, and now know I'm equipped with the right skills to overcome any obstacle. I strongly recommend anyone to read any of the books about The Three Principles. Sometimes it can just be one line or even one word, and nothing will ever be the same for you again … I wish all the best to people on their journeys — **don't ever give up and keep an open heart** [emphasis added].

Our True Nature

When we have a life-changing experience like the girl in the previous story, what we really begin to *remember* is our own true nature. In other words, we actually reactivate the vibrant mental health, wisdom, and well-being we were *all* born with. This kind of transformation is possible for all of us, and can occur at any moment, because it is our birthright. This is possible, despite the fact that we may not have had a healthy and advantageous childhood. As a consequence of our shift in consciousness, we more deeply comprehend that the world that we experience is created by the moment-to-moment magic of our thoughts. Isn't that amazing? This experience we call our life is miraculously coming from the inside out. This Great Remembering turns the world, *our* world, the right way around, the way it is meant to be. And this helps us intuitively cope with life's ups and downs, and begin to thrive with our newfound resilience and strength of spirit.

Bored, Bored, Bored!

The experience of boredom is not something that happens *to* us, it is a feeling we get when we have a certain set of thoughts. Neither is boredom a *thing*; it is simply an experience we create from our thinking about the things we find tedious. Life will probably always present us with situations that we find laborious, that we would rather not do. This could be in a classroom during a lesson we struggle with. Or, it could be with a teacher we find particularly boring due to the way they deliver the material. However, whatever the circumstances we're in, we often arrive with a fixed mindset about how the lesson is going to be. With these preconceived ideas of how *boring* it *will* be. We may start thinking: "This lesson is really dragging on! I would much rather be at break (recess) with my friends, or at home doing the things I love to do! Why do we even study this stuff anyway? When am I ever going to use this when I leave school? This is just a waste of my time."

All these thoughts ultimately lead to feelings of dissatisfaction, which, in our mind, we name 'boredom'. The lesson appears to be 'boring' because we are having those particular thoughts that we would rather be somewhere else, doing something else. Thus, it looks like the feelings of our boredom are coming from the outside, from the teacher or the lesson itself. When, in fact, these uncomfortable feelings are coming from the thoughts we are having about the situation we are in at the time. Despite the fact that a teacher may struggle to impart the learning in a clear and helpful way; if we are determined to learn, we will discover the right information anyway. Especially, when we understand our part in these feelings of 'boredom', because we will have a clearer mind, which always helps us learn in a very natural way.

For most of us, our foremost desire is to have an enjoyable life, and to be okay and to thrive. And so when we are feeling things are not going according to our plan to enjoy life, we probably feel we want to be somewhere other than in our present circumstances. From this, we may make the assumption that if we were free of our current task, we would automatically be happier. However, our happiness is not dependent on what we are doing or not doing, happiness comes from within; from the thoughts we are having about life in the moment. When we can *see* more clearly the role thought is actually playing in our feelings of boredom, it is much more difficult to look on all tasks and activities as anything but what they are; an action that requires our attention for a period of time. I remember being fascinated after reading about a tribe that lived deep in the Amazon jungle, that didn't have a word in their language for work! They just went about their day, doing whatever tasks needed to be done, and most of these undertakings they simply did joyously! What a difference one single thought can make, knowing this alone can set us free from the uncomfortable feelings, and we will probably feel 'bored', a lot less of the time.

Bullying

(Please note if you are being bullied, for your own safety, it is important to speak to somebody, either at school or home or call the bullying helpline number in your country. This should be available online.)

Bullying can take on many forms; it can be physical, verbal, social, or cyber. But whatever form it takes it is worth keeping in mind that it is not coming from a place of love and understanding. People we call bullies are usually unhappy themselves.

Often people seem to think that it is wrong to talk about bad behaviour, and to report what they have witnessed of psychological teasing or physical bullying. At times, it may be because people fear they will get bullied too. Other times, it could simply be because modern culture leads some of us to believe that reporting a wrongdoing is dishonest in itself! In other words people seem to think that to 'grass', 'snitch' or 'dob' someone into teachers, parents or authorities is just not socially acceptable. This notion that it is wrong to 'do the right thing' is irrational, so how can we get past this 'sticky' problem?

'Bullying' is a nasty habit that some people get into, and is often a strong indication that things are not going well in the bully's life! The individual bully may even be being picked on themselves. Society tends to label a person as a bully when they are seen to act in a bullying manner often enough for most people to notice. Bullying can happen anywhere, at school, at home and even out in society. And it can take the form of physical harm or psychological abuse. The first thing we must do in either case is to seek help, so that we can prevent the bullying from continuing, or even getting worse.

Despite the fact that it is an awful thing to be on the receiving end of a bully's attacks, it is also worth remembering that when a person is acting in this way, it is probably because they are suffering deeply too. How do we know they are suffering? The simple logic of this is that when we are in a friendly mood and feeling cheerful and confident in ourselves, it is almost impossible to treat others in an unkind or unfriendly manner. If this is true for us, then it must be true for everyone, even those doing the bullying.

Psychological or mental bullying can sometimes start out with what the bully might think of as innocent teasing or peer pressure. The bully may come from a home where this type of intimidating behaviour is an everyday occurrence. And so, the bully may see and *think* this way of acting towards others is just a normal part of life, rather than seeing their actions as causing harm. However, when someone has not yet remembered that thought creates reality, this experience of being 'teased' by a bully, can feel very painful and frightening for the victim. Sometimes, as a result of this type of bullying, the sufferers may start to hide within themselves, and become less outgoing, in fear of being bullied by others. This withdrawal may lead to intensely unhappy feelings of despair, and self-worthlessness, and this can sometimes lead to self-harm. In the worst case, individuals can end up feeling so unhappy about their lives that they decide it isn't worth living! This is such a terrible waste of a beautiful life. Not one single person should ever have to die because of the teasing and bullying behaviour of others.

One simple way to help to prevent bullying from happening is by showing kindness to each other. An old saying suggests, "A little bit of kindness goes a long way". And it may well be just the thing a suffering person needs in order to feel better within themselves. This is the same for victims of bullying and for the bully too. Once we calm down and start having nicer thoughts and feelings about ourselves, things get easier for most of us. However, sometimes speaking up about bullying is what is needed.

Physical bullying is much more obvious in that it can be witnessed in action, and sometimes the evidence of physical violence is visible on the wounded. This kind of bullying can also take on a subtle form, in that the bully only causes harm, when they *think* that no one is watching. People who have been physically hurt, at home or elsewhere, may end up becoming a bully, because they feel angry at the world for the violence they have suffered. Though, this is not always the case; sometimes people are just put off by life and fed up with their circumstances. From this unhappy thinking about life, they innocently 'strike out' at the world and whoever happens to be in the way, may get hurt. This, of course, doesn't make this vicious behaviour okay.

However, it is worth keeping in mind that despite falling victim to violence, it is our wiser thoughts about what has happened, that will allow us to regain our birthright of self-confidence. Our wisdom and common sense will often lead us to get ourselves out of the firing line of the bully, and seek safety and help. Additionally, as our confidence and self assurance begins to return we might simply stand up for ourselves in a way that even surprise us. We do not become the victim of violence because of *who we are*, we simply get caught in the cross fire of a person lost in anger. We all get angry from time to time, but when we remember that anger stems from our thinking, it becomes easier to not take our anger so seriously or to take it out on others.

In the End, Only Kindness Matters

"At the end of the day people won't remember what you said or did, they will remember how you made them feel." Maya Angelou

Most of us tend to gravitate toward people that we love being around, because of how we feel when we are with them. Our thinking becomes easier and lighter when we don't have to second-guess what a person may say or do. These are the people whom we trust without question, and this allows us to more easily treat them with kindness when they are having a difficult day themselves.

However, in life we will all come across people that are suffering and unhappy in their lives. If we can find it in our hearts to offer our kindness to these people too, it can make a real difference to their day. And our kindness can also help these people begin to *remember* and see the role of thought in the creation of their feelings. It is often the case, that people who act in an unkind manner towards us, or toward others are suffering themselves. If we remember where their suffering is coming from, it is easier for us to help them too. Kindness can become contagious.

Living in our Very Own Bubble

Our thoughts and feelings are totally unique to us. Therefore, only we can ever fully understand and appreciate the true essence of who we are. We create a unique life all of our own and we live in our own self-made world, our very own bubble. Some call this our 'separate reality'. Other people around us can only get a peek into our lives when we share our world with them. As has been mentioned before, we are the world's best expert on ourselves! Nobody will ever know us like we do. This is extraordinary, but true.

I met a young man when he was thirteen years old. He had been in foster care since he was ten years old. During this time, I had the good fortune to take him to training sessions with my mentor, the late Dr. Roger Mills. The young man and I spent time together over many years, and he would sometimes get in a muddle with his thinking, as we all do. Usually, if we had a good chat, which often involved a lot of laughter, things got easier for him.

There were many things that he felt he couldn't do in life, but over time he regained his self-confidence, and gave them a try. He discovered that he had a good supply of natural ability to use his mind in new ways, and if he put the effort in he got good results. Over the years, he gained much more self-assurance and boldness in himself and racked up a degree in Business Studies at University of East London. Now he is a powerful advocate for the thousands of young people who leave care every year in the UK. One day out of the blue, I received a beautiful message from him. Here is an excerpt from what he wrote:

> ... *So that 13-year old boy who started to realise he created his own reality is turning into a man, hopefully continuing to bring into existence a positive reality for himself and others; this is what I want to do really, deeply and truly! And you are the person who put me on that path, you showed me the first step and that will never be forgotten!*
>
> *You're the man who helped me shake Ian Duncan Smith's hand* [UK Secretary of State for Work and Pensions] *yesterday after he heard my representation of those 10,000 children who leave care every single year. We are now on the radar of the* [UK Government] *Cabinet Office, we can actually have our voices heard, so we are in for a real chance of moving away from being segregated from society and treated as a minority or a problem that needs to be swept under the rug and ignored! Thank you.*
>
> *The Three Principles rooted my mind and my heart back to its natural state. From which every day I manage to grow and resonate from with others ...*

Vacation Land (the Holiday State)

Many of us may have had the thought: It would be *so* good to be on holiday all of the time! This dream of an easeful, relaxing life, laying around in the sun, eating good food, and spending oodles of time doing all the things we love to do, is totally understandable. Yet, when we are living day to day, going to school and being busy in life, moving from one thing to the next without much let up, our thinking can crowd up on us. But whether we are busy or just 'hanging out', we can still have a mind full of the busy thoughts of life. When we do have a head full of troubling thoughts, or even feeling bored with life, it becomes much harder to be present, and enjoy the precious moments of our lives. That is, until we start to remember the role our state of mind plays in the living of our everyday lives.

To relax while we are on holiday is somehow an obvious thing to experience, it's a 'no brainer', and so we take it for granted when this happens. Yet, what we often fail to notice is that it is a subtle but powerful shift in our thinking that creates the good feelings we experience, not the change in circumstances and environment. Put simply, when we are on holiday, we generally have less on our minds; we don't tend to think about school, or any of life's dramas and upsets. We 'let loose' and have a party, and therefore it is natural for us to experience a deeper state of emotional health. When we are in a calmer state of mind and feeling more relaxed, this makes it easier to remember who we are. And we may wonder why we don't feel like this more of the time. The great news is, that we can; it is very possible to live in that holiday feeling more of the time.

We could be back at school, or doing homework assignments, washing the dishes after dinner, doing chores around the house, or even cleaning our room, and yet still be experiencing nicer feelings. This is possible because *our feelings don't come from what we are doing, they are generated from our thinking ABOUT the chores of life*. This experience of nicer feelings becomes so much more possible when we understand the infinite part that thought plays in our emotional state. We begin to see that living more and more of our lives in that holiday feeling is possible because our cheerfulness does not depend on the things we are engaged in. Our happiness is only 'one thought away' from wherever we are right now in our thinking.

Change like the Weather

One of the amazing things about thinking is that it can change as quickly as the weather. Thinking can be just like a sunny day in the tropics, which suddenly begins to throw down rain in buckets. One moment we can be feeling fine, and the next our thoughts and feelings can become stormy like a torrent. There are times in life when our circumstances lead to the development of unhappy thoughts and feelings. When I was younger, my brother phoned to tell me our family dog had just died. However calm my thinking was before the call, I could barely speak for crying about the loss of our dearly loved dog. Naturally, my thinking took a nose dive and my emotions sunk to a low space. As we all know, these feeling usually subside, when we get used to the fact of the loss, and it is different for each of us. It is not that we *overcome* the pain; our low emotional state passes as our thoughts settle once again.

Also, we can end up in difficult situations where we might be having a disagreement with someone, or we are in danger of being hurt. At these times, our feelings may drop very low as our mind rushes to find a solution. However, even when these more difficult and uncomfortable situations arise, our common sense will tell us to 'beat a hasty retreat' and guides us back to safety. And when we find ourselves in circumstances that are calmer and safer, our thinking will ease up and so will our feelings.

While a teacher at high school, I often used to ask the question: "Can anyone give an example of something that *doesn't* come from thought?" In response to this question, a boy suggested the following. He said that that he had been in the playground talking to some friends when someone came up behind him and slapped him on the back of the head. He continued: "I didn't *think*, I just turned around and hit the boy back, and then I got in trouble!" When we discussed this as a class, I suggested that if the boy hadn't been *thinking*, then he wouldn't have even noticed that he had been hit! This is because without thought being present, nothing can register in the mind.

After some laughter, we discussed the lightening speed at which thought takes place, and how it is impossible to really stop thoughts from occurring. Thinking changes from moment to moment, but it is not the content of our thinking that is a problem, it is the fact that we can think, and *which* thoughts we focus on. Because the thoughts we give our energy to create the living experience of the moment. And the more we understand this, the easier it will become to ride out the storms of life. This does not mean to say that all our problems magically disappear; it is that we become more capable of dealing with them when they arrive.

Moods

Everyone we know has moods, good moods, bad moods, sad moods, silly moods and every kind of mood we can think of. Yet, it is important for us to remember where moods come from. A mood is simply the way we describe how we are feeling. All feelings come from the way we think. Therefore moods come from our habits of thinking. Moods are less of a problem to us when we remember where they come from, because we know they will not last. Thankfully, this really helps when we notice others in a low mood, because we can become more accepting, knowing this too will not last. Sometimes, we may even be able to help a person get past their low mood thinking just by being naturally happy around them. Good feelings tend to be contagious.

Anxiety

We all feel worried and upset from time to time, and occasionally these uneasy feelings can lead to a state of deep anxiety and a lot of fear. We can start to fear going outside alone, or being in crowds. Some find it difficult to go to school, or travel in elevators. Some people feel they can't travel on public transport, or fly. Others only feel safe when they are with friends or family.

Anxiety can appear in countless ways because our experience of anxiety comes from our unique conditioning via our thinking. Put another way, when we are in an anxious state of mind, our experience is made up of our nervous thinking about circumstances, as we look at them through the lenses of the past. Sometimes, we may think that anxiety is a 'thing', when in fact; it is created within us, with our thoughts. A state of anxiety cannot exist outside of our thinking, because it is only made up of thought! When we stop having these fearful thoughts, the feelings disappear as quickly as they arrived.

There is of course, 'natural fear', sometimes called 'fight or flight', or an 'adrenaline response', which we are all born with. This natural fear is what helps us to get out of dangerous or life threatening situations; it is what we might call an instinctual response to a threat. Yet, our 'fight or flight' response can also be triggered in other situations too, such as worry or fear before an important event such as an exam or presentation.

What is interesting about natural fear is that we may have been through something painful or frightening in the past, which left a deep impression on our mind in the form of a memory. This memory can pop back up in our thinking and create similar feelings to a past experience. This can happen even when the situation is not truly dangerous. These situations can create an impression in us that something is *wrong*, even though the circumstances are not related. These feelings are thought carried through time, and as we gently remember this, we tend to experience less anxious feelings in life. The secret to feeling less anxious lies in the magic of thought.

> *When I was a small boy of ten years old, around a year or so after my mother had died, I didn't like my life at home too much and wanted to run away. I felt that life was cruel and hard and that there must be something better out there in the world for me. I planned my escape, got a few things together and thought I could hide out somewhere until I was forgotten. I was so deeply unhappy; that I felt running away would take away my unhappy feelings. Luckily for my family, and me, something inside me said: "Don't do it! Things will only get worse. They will find you and bring you back, then things will be really bad." So I stayed. This voice inside was my natural intelligence, wisdom or common sense, which guides us all through life, if we get quiet enough to hear where it is guiding us. Thankfully, in that moment, I was listening to my wisdom. We don't have to be taught wisdom. We just know it intuitively inside ourselves and it arises in a way that is unique to us.*

Each one of us has a totally distinctive life and circumstances in which we live, and we must decide what is best for us. It is difficult to trust our thinking when we are feeling low. But one way of being certain that our decision is coming from our wisdom is that it always, always comes with a good feeling. This feeling is a lighter feeling, a feeling of relief, an 'aha'! moment, which is wisdom popping into our minds. When this 'aha' moment happens we simply *know* the right course to take, with absolute certainty. Wisdom sits outside of time, and we only have to have a fraction of a second gap in our low mood thinking, for wisdom to fill the space with a clear and certain answer and that lighter feeling we get inside.

Self-Harm & Body Image

Some people get so upset with the circumstances of their lives that they start to harm themselves. This can be for many reasons: body image and size, how good a person feels about themselves, perhaps how they are doing at school, or it could be motivated by what others say about them. Most of the time, this physical harm is never so bad that the person could die, but it can be bad enough to cause injury and scarring or damage to the body, and will probably upset and frighten family and friends.

It seems that often, self-harm is a way for an individual to momentarily take away the bad feelings they are living with. This could be likened to a stark form of distraction; replacing emotional or psychological suffering with some kind of physical pain. And so the pain of the self-harm becomes a diversion from the agony of living with negative thoughts and bad feelings. When a person starts to see with more clarity that thought *creates all feelings*, it is easier for them to start to feel better about themselves. They begin to remember how life works, and to understand that their self-harm has its source in their innocently 'off track' thinking. Accepting this usually helps people stop self-harming and return to nicer feelings and kinder thoughts about themselves and life in general. Because they see that the negative thoughts they have been having about themselves are not real or true. Ultimately, everyone wants to feel like they fit in somewhere in life. And the kinder our thoughts are towards ourselves, the calmer our mind becomes. When a person's thinking shifts, they begin to feel at home with who they are, which makes life much more enjoyable to be part of, knowing that they are really okay from within.

Sex, Drugs & Rock & Roll

Almost every adult-themed movie we watch contains one of the following: someone drinking, smoking or taking drugs, *especially* when things are going wrong for the characters in the story.

This spreads the lie that society keeps telling us, that we need something from the *outside* to feel better when things go wrong in our lives. As we have seen throughout this little book, all feelings come from within. They come from what we are thinking about, and so we begin to realise that the way to better feelings is to not think about the tough stuff anymore; not put energy into it. This is not to say that we deny the circumstances of our lives. If we find we are in trouble or danger, we need to look after ourselves and seek safety and help. However, we can lighten up and take it easy on ourselves. The real reason people seem to feel better when under the influence of substances is because they are already capable of having those good feelings without the alcohol or drugs. It is good to remember that nicer feelings are a natural part of who we are; in fact they are our birthright and come from deep within us, and occur quite naturally from our innate mental health.

Ultimately, addiction is not about a chemical dependency. It is the desire to rid ourselves of negative and painful thinking. We feel better about life and ourselves when we truly and deeply see how *thought* creates the life and the feeling we live in. We are not born with a need for drugs or alcohol in our body. Each one of us including everyone else in the world is born with all we need to have a happy and healthy life from the inside out.

Conclusion

This book is designed to point us all in one direction only. It is designed to help us to look within for our own answers so we learn to trust our own wisdom. As we do this, we begin to understand that:

- We have as much common sense and wisdom as anyone else.
- Whatever we have been told by others, we are whole, undamaged, and we have natural intelligence inside of us.
- We too can live a great life, despite what has happened to us in our past.
- We all have an unbreakable spirit within us, which can never be damaged, diminished or worn out.

- This spirit we are born with is the same in everyone and connects us to all life.
- We are the world's best experts on ourselves and no-one can ever know us as well as we know ourselves.
- We have unlimited psychological potential as a person.
- We create our own life through the thoughts we carry in our heads.
- We can have the best life ever. All we need is to remember who and what we really are, and how we create our own reality via thought.

You are one amazing person; so don't be shy about shining for the world! The world is a much better place with your beauty and unique magic in it. Shine on and share the joys of the Great Remembering with everyone you meet: because every beautiful soul in this world deserves to live the best life ever.

Now, go and have a wonderful life, for it is just one thought away...

Acknowledgments

Firstly my warmest thanks go out to all the wonderful young people I had the privilege to work with over the many years I enjoyed as a teacher, as this book would not have even come into being without your stories and my connection with you all. Thank you for all you have shared with me.

Secondly I would like to thank everyone who gave their time to reading early manuscripts, and for their editing advice and guidance, especially Lisa Leslie, and Natalie Stockdale. My heartfelt thanks go out to my American sister Ami Chen Mills-Niam for her astute editing and advice for this little book. Also a special mention must go to Jessica Procopio for her close reading and excellent feedback on the text. Additionally, my heartfelt thanks goes to Kathy Divine for the final push to get this book out into the world and made available for teens the world over.

About The Author

Dean Rees-Evans MSc is a Human Relations Consultant, Teacher, Researcher, Trainer, Wellbeing Mentor and International Public Speaker. After completing his undergraduate degree in English and Drama, Dean worked in high school education, with a variety of students, including special needs, troubled youth, young offenders, and those excluded from mainstream education. Dean received his MSc after conducting a successful research pilot study at a UK high school. Establishing Three Principles: Well-Being for Life in 2005 he mentors individuals, groups, families, and teenagers and conducts training and consulting with schools, hospitals and businesses.

Connect with Dean Rees-Evans

Dean Rees-Evans runs inspiring and life-changing workshops, offers dynamic individual and group coaching and holds exciting events. Connect with Dean via social media and his website to keep informed about his work.

facebook.com/ThreePrinciplesTraining

https://bit.ly/3eadE1n

threeprinciples.com.au

Printed in Great Britain
by Amazon